teacher's friend publications

Kindergarten Basic Skills

Visual Perception, Classifying, and Cut and Paste

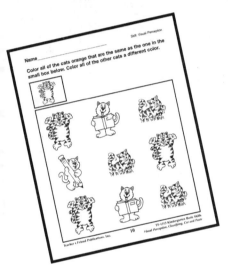

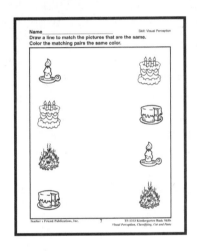

Basic early learning activities necessary for developing the skills students need to succeed!

Written by: Aaron Levy & Kelley Wingate Levy
Illustrated by: Karen Sevaly

Look for all of Teacher's Friend's Basic Skills Books at your local educational retailer!

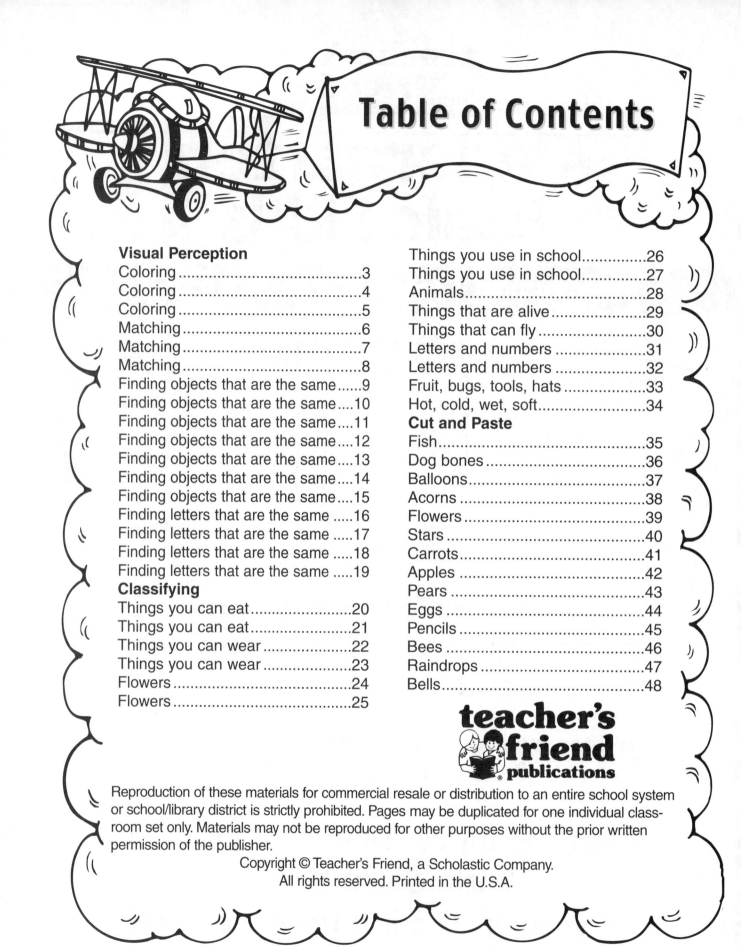

Table of Contents

teacher's friend publications

ISBN-13 978-0-439-50029-6
ISBN-10 0-439-50029-X

Color the objects below. Use the color key.

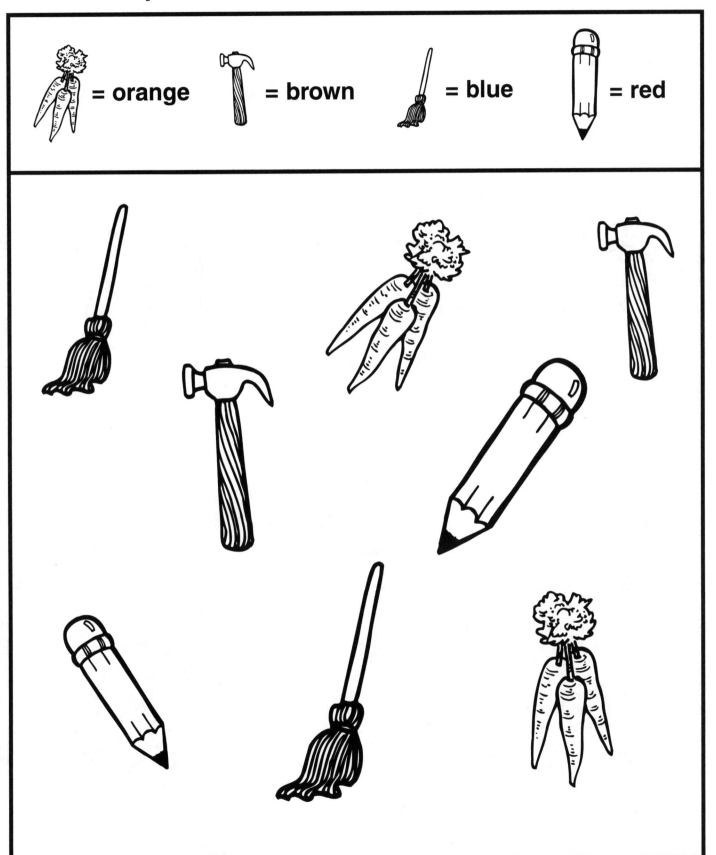

= orange   = brown   = blue   = red

Color the objects below. Use the color key.

 = **orange**    = **blue**   = **red**

Name_____

Color the objects below. Use the color key.

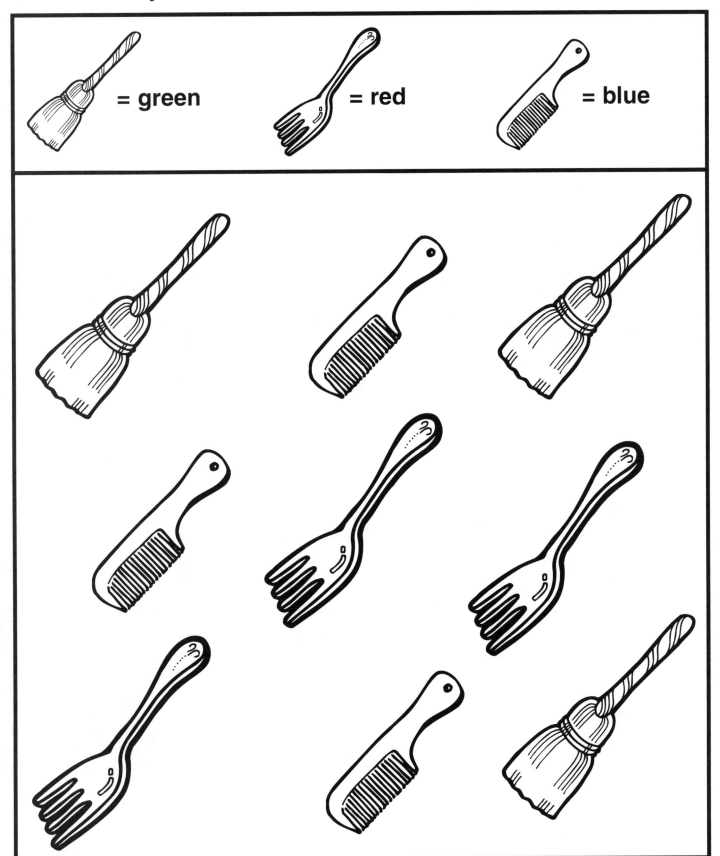

= green

= red

= blue

Draw a line to match the pictures that are the same. Color the matching pairs the same color.

Name_____

Draw a line to match the pictures that are the same.
Color the matching pairs the same color.

Draw a line to match the pictures that are the same.
Color the matching pairs the same color.

Color the hats brown that are the same as the one in the small box below. Color all of the other hats a different color.

Color all of the cats orange that are the same as the one in the small box below. Color all of the other cats a different color.

Color all of the girls red that are the same as the one in the small box below. Color all of the other girls a different color.

Name_____

Circle and color the objects that are the same in each box.

12

Circle and color the objects that are the same in each box.

Name_____

Circle and color the objects that are the same in each row.

Circle and color the objects that are the same as the first object.

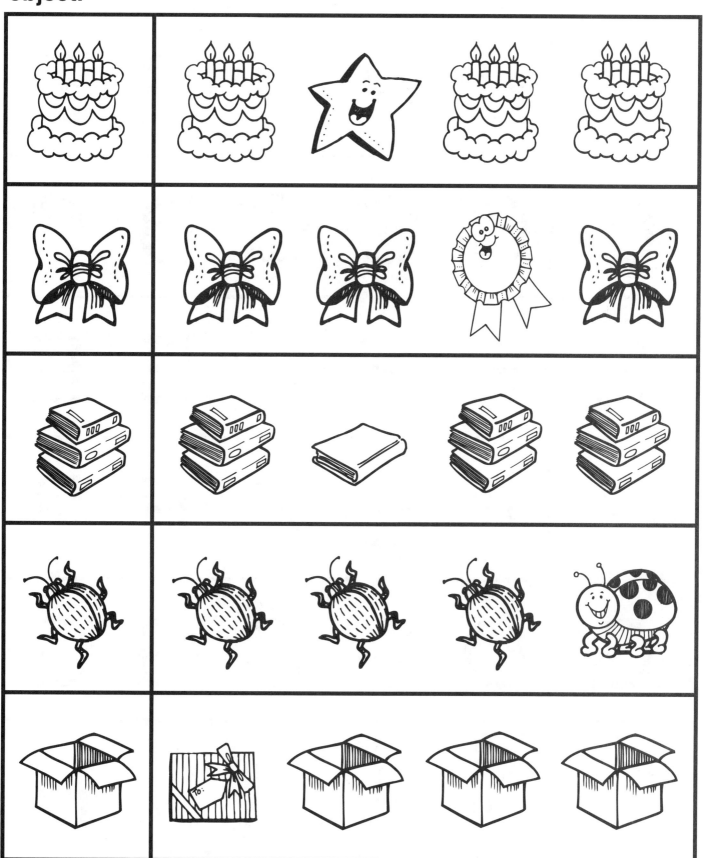

Visual Perception, Classifying, Cut and Paste

Name_____

In each row, circle the letters that are the same as the first letter.

B	B P B R B
C	O C C D C
E	E F B E E
F	F E F F P
G	O G C G G
M	N W M M M

Name_____

In each row, circle the letters that are the same as the first letter.

O	C O O O D
P	P P R B P
Q	C Q Q O Q
R	B R P R R
U	U U V W U
V	U V V V W

TF-1313 Kindergarten Basic Skills
Visual Perception, Classifying, Cut and Paste

In each row, circle the letters that are the same as the first letter.

a	a a d o a
b	b p d b b
c	o c c c a
d	b d a d d
m	m m m n r
n	h n m n n

Name_____

In each row, circle the letters that are the same as the first letter.

o	o c o a o
p	d p p p b
q	q g p q q
u	v u u w u
v	v v u w v
w	w w w u v

Circle and color the objects that you can eat.

Circle and color the objects that you can eat.

Circle and color the objects that you can wear.

Circle and color the objects that you can wear.

Circle and color the flowers.

Circle and color the flowers.

Circle and color the items that you might use in school.

Name_____

Circle and color the items that you might use in school.

TF-1313 Kindergarten Basic Skills
Visual Perception, Classifying, Cut and Paste

Circle and color the animals.

Draw a circle around the pictures of things that are alive.
Draw an X through the pictures of things that are not alive.

Visual Perception, Classifying, Cut and Paste

Name_____

Draw a circle around the pictures of things that can fly.
Draw an X through the pictures of things that cannot fly.

Skill: Classifying

Draw a circle around each number.
Draw an X through each letter.

1	P	8	6
10	T	L	G
C	2	Y	7
O	X	3	H
4	W	2	T
A	5	B	9

TF-1313 Kindergarten Basic Skills
Visual Perception, Classifying, Cut and Paste

Name_____

Draw a circle around each number.
Draw an X through each letter.

7	p	f	1
h	2	10	k
s	n	5	a
4	d	o	9
y	r	3	m
8	t	b	6

32

Name_____

Under each picture, write which group that picture belongs to. Use the words listed below.

fruit	bug	tool	hat

_____

_____

_____

_____

_____

_____

_____

_____

_____

TF-1313 Kindergarten Basic Skills
Visual Perception, Classifying, Cut and Paste

Under each picture, write which group that picture belongs to. Use the words listed below.

hot	cold	wet	soft

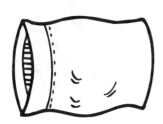

TF-1313 Kindergarten Basic Skills
Visual Perception, Classifying, Cut and Paste

Name_____

Cut out the pictures at the bottom of the page and paste them in the correct space.

Visual Perception, Classifying, Cut and Paste

Name_____

Cut out the pictures at the bottom of the page and paste them in the correct space.

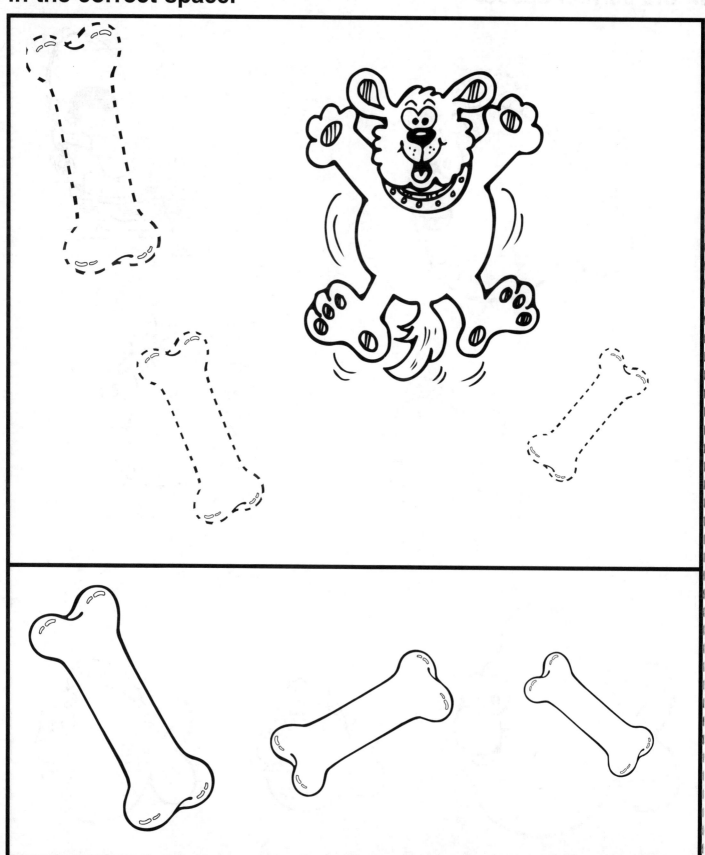

36

Name_____

Cut out the pictures at the bottom of the page and paste them in the correct space.

Name_____

Cut out the pictures at the bottom of the page and paste them in the correct space.

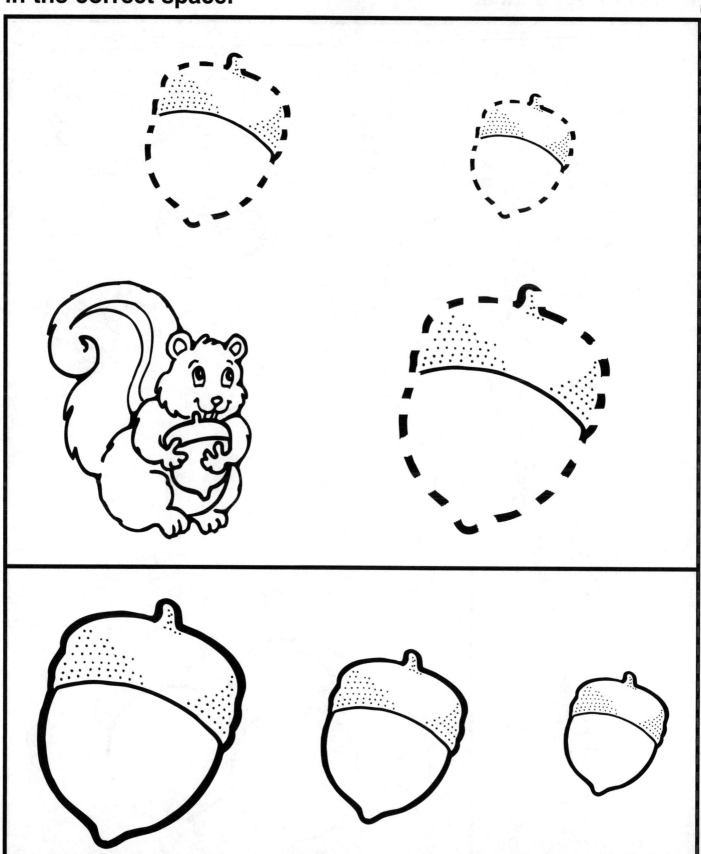

Visual Perception, Classifying, Cut and Paste

Name_____

Cut out the pictures at the bottom of the page and paste them in the correct space.

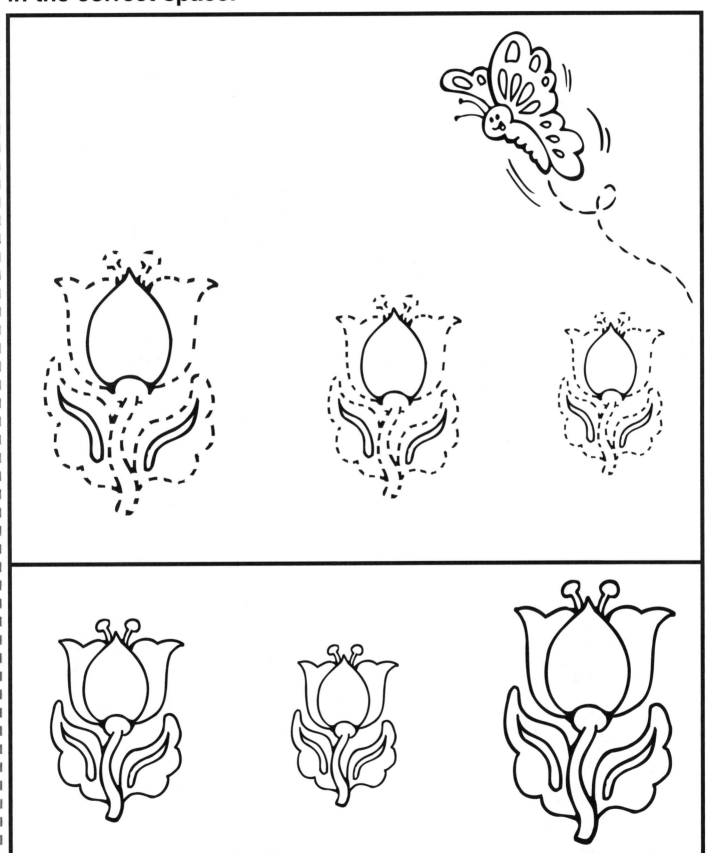

Cut out the pictures at the bottom of the page and paste them in the correct space.

Cut out the pictures at the bottom of the page and paste them in the correct space.

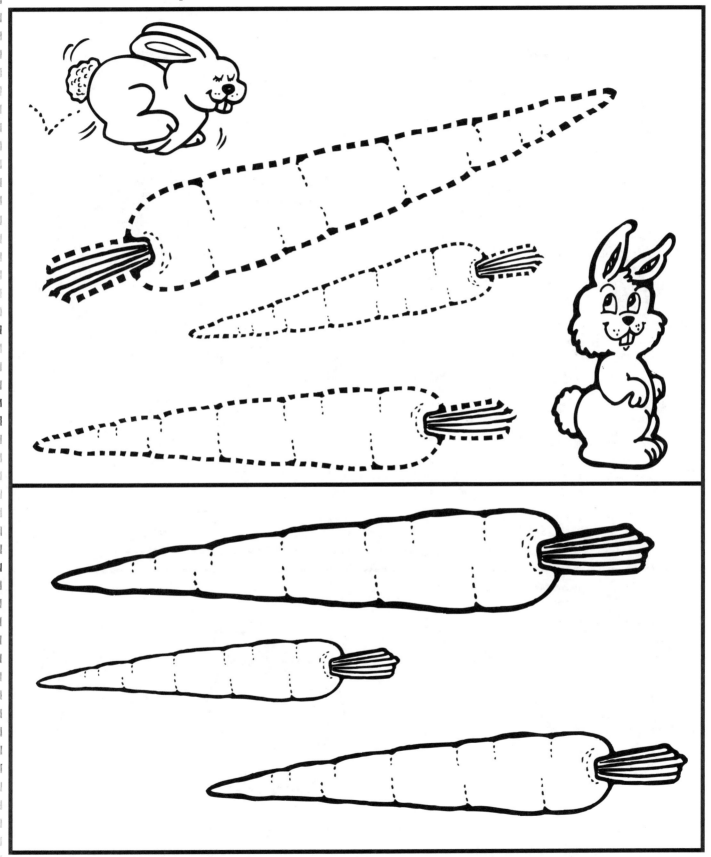

Name_____

Cut out the pictures at the bottom of the page and paste them in the correct space.

TF-1313 Kindergarten Basic Skills
Visual Perception, Classifying, Cut and Paste

Cut out the pictures at the bottom of the page and paste them in the correct space.

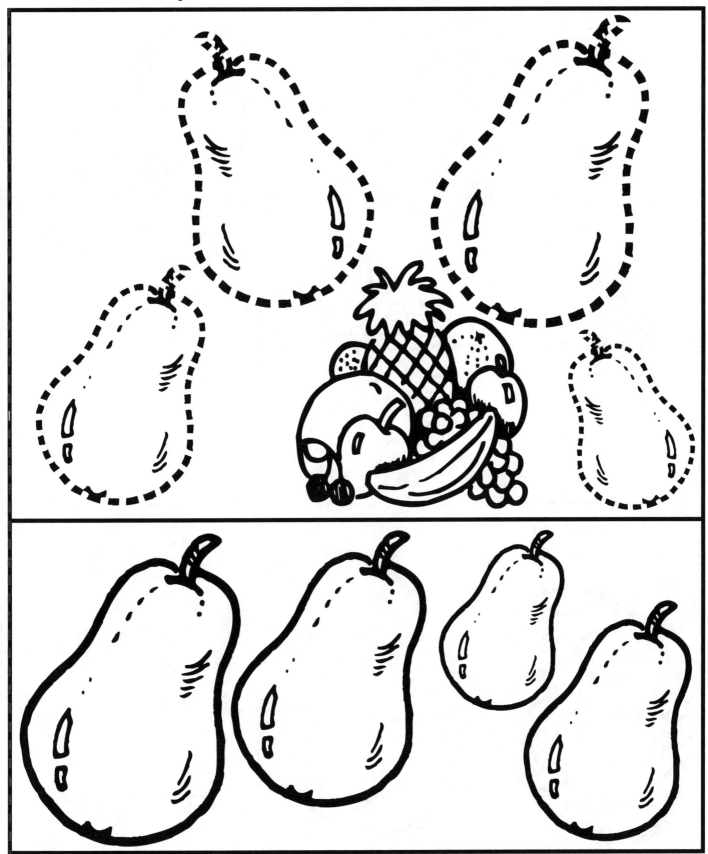

43

Name_____

Cut out the pictures at the bottom of the page and paste them in the correct space.

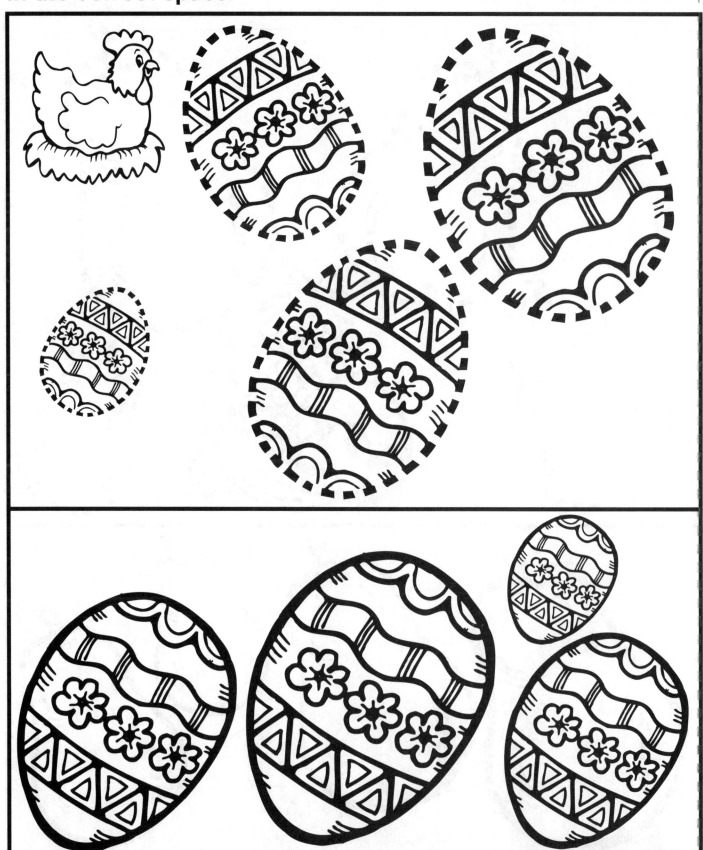

Visual Perception, Classifying, Cut and Paste

Name_____

Cut out the pictures at the bottom of the page and paste them in the correct space.

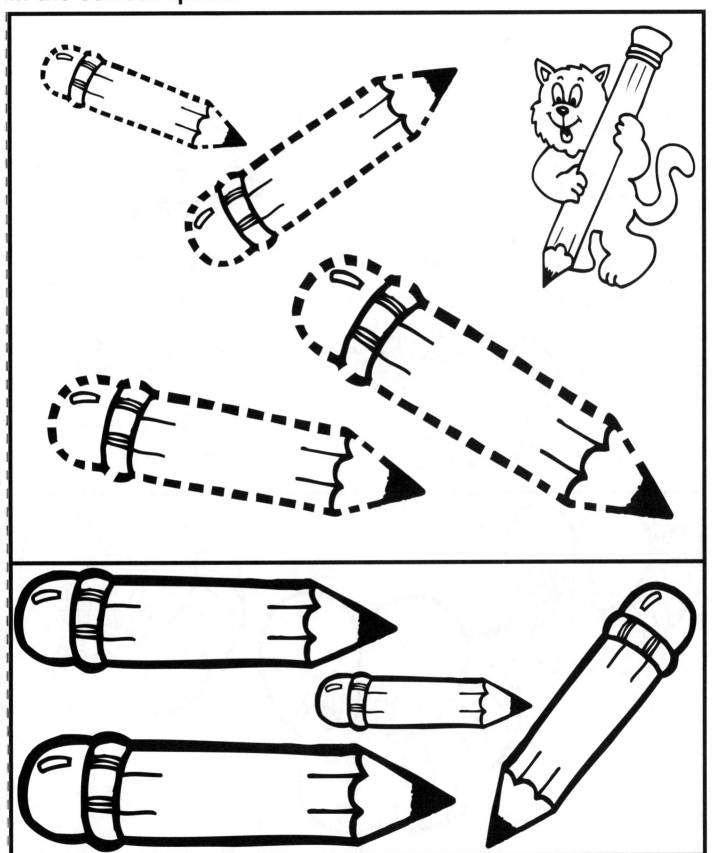

Cut out the pictures at the bottom of the page and paste them in the correct space.

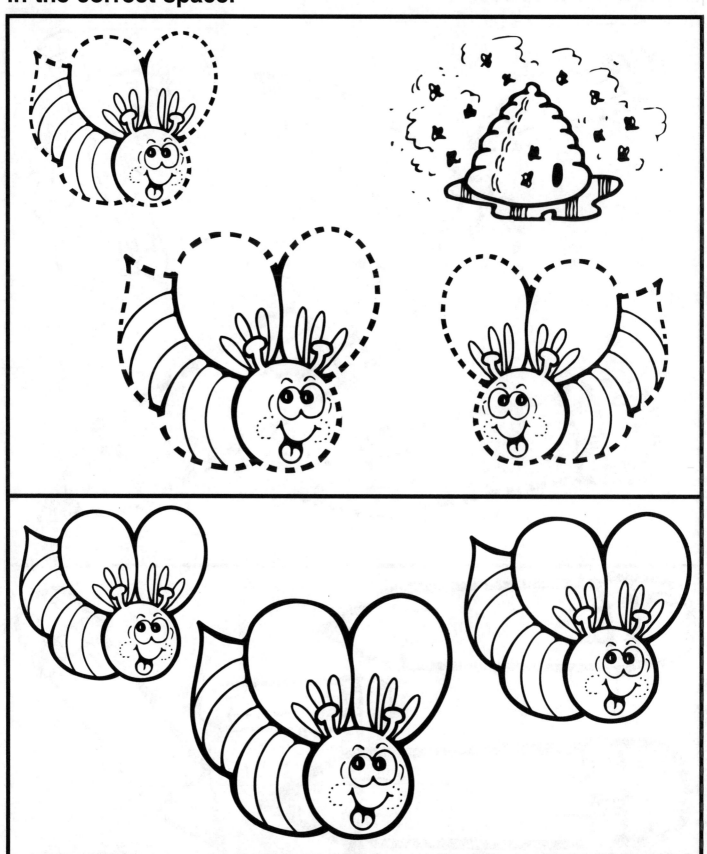

Name_____

Cut out the pictures at the bottom of the page and paste them in the correct space.

47

Name_____

Cut out the pictures at the bottom of the page and paste them in the correct space.

Visual Perception, Classifying, Cut and Paste